"In this collection of poetry, Harold Recinos inhabits the world of those that live on the edge of society, the migrants that cross rivers at nighttime to find refuge in a land that often turns them back. Recinos speaks of the inherent racism that people—Brown people, women, emigrants—experience in America, and he does it with extraordinary depth and beauty. This is an extraordinary collection of poems that will break your heart and inspire change in our fragmented world."

—MARJORIE AGOSIN,
author of the Pura Belpré Award–winning *I Lived on Butterfly Hill*

"Seemingly drawing inspiration from the likes of Whitman, Neruda, and Cardenal, *The Looking Glass: Far and Near* lifts up the voices of the dispossessed and abandoned Central Americans, Puerto Ricans, Mexicans, and other Brown people with prophetic and poetic moral indignation. This moving book of poetry brings forth faith and hope despite the last would-be tyrant's efforts to destroy democracy and join a heartless world."

—GREG DAWES,
author of *Pablo Neruda's Poetry and Politics*

"Each poem takes us step by step beyond the dehumanizing rush of modernity in search of paradise lost. In a world burdened by technology, climate change, and hate, this collection offers the reader a moment of simplicity, beauty, and love."

—LINDA M. RODRÍGUEZ GUGLIELMONI,
author of *En barco de papel: La aventura de María Angelina y su papa Eugenio María de Hostos.*

"Harold Recinos is the fierce and relentless theologian of the Bronx's barrios and bodegas. He is the poet laureate of First Avenue and Spanglish. These poems bear witness to his immigrant community and show us the lives of those who live at the margins of hope."

—DONALD PLATT,
author of *Swansdown*

"Rather than dwell in nostalgia, these poems ask us to consider how the present can be made better by the lessons of the past and by careful study of the moment—of human voices and the intricacy of their 'inexhaustible light.' Harold Recinos has written song of hope for the present. Sit with this marvel. You will be better for it."

—RODNEY GOMEZ,
author of *Arsenal with Praise Song.*

The Looking Glass

The Looking Glass

Far and Near

HAROLD J. RECINOS

RESOURCE *Publications* · Eugene, Oregon

THE LOOKING GLASS
Far and Near

Resource Publications
An Imprint of Wipf and Stock Publishers
199 W. 8th Ave., Suite 3
Eugene, OR 97401

www.wipfandstock.com

PAPERBACK ISBN: 978-1-6667-5790-3
HARDCOVER ISBN: 978-1-6667-5791-0
EBOOK ISBN: 978-1-6667-5792-7

01/05/23

Contents

SIMPLICITY

I recall a time when life was
simple, knotless, uncomplicated
and occupied by hop scotch, round
up tag, stick ball on the street
and subway rides to Manhattan
for the hell of it. the first day
of the public-school week never
failed to find its way to Friday
when most of the block kids found
themselves in Margarita's apartment
for a little night of salsa and floating
dreams. where did that simplicity
come from, perhaps the candles left
burning by mothers in the local Catholic
church, charms from the Ponce Botanica
worn around our skinny necks, stories
from Spanish lands holding us by the
hand to prevent shattering or the long
conversations with the old men of the
block that made us laugh. I recall days
when we were free of the fallacies of
modernity, the distortions of detestable
politics, nights were spent on the roof
top looking at the moon exhaling silvery
light and feelings of consolation were
abundant.

TWILIGHT

I am at sitting at a table in
a tiny café with the usual
early evening English and
Spanish thoughts chasing
each other in me. the sky
is kissing daytime good
night, the twilight bells
of the church across the
street begin to ring and I
see two slim Puerto Rican
boys on the corner with a
small crowd around them
break-dancing for cash. as
the earth spins on its titled
axis, unexpected sweets and
treasures like these glorify
happiness just because they
must. the most beautiful thing
about the moment is taking the
time to roam the coming dusk
so full of beauty that death and
sadness dare not enter it. who
knows, maybe tonight I will
see the brief streaking light of
a shooting star and wish to sit
here forever.

MEDITATION

they asked him once in
the barrio how his life is
joined to history at the edges
of the city and the eyes on the
block no longer able to hold
tears. they held his calloused
hands in church to pray, his
tongue did not move and his
thoughts were occupied by
the impossibility of salvation.
they wanted to know what it
felt like to hold a teen boy who
walked all night to reach him
to die in his arms. he said time
had become wordless sadness
and like hoarse water swallowed
under a frightening sky. I always
run into him sitting on the stoop
waiting for something, looking up
and down the street, sometimes even
up at heaven, searching I think for
signs of chariots swinging low.

NAKED CITY

I am going to walk down Fifth Avenue
today from the library to Houston Street
and make a turn toward the east until I
get down to Avenue D. along the way
I plan to keep my eyes wide open just in
case the Holy Ghost is bent over trash
cans on the corners fishing out plastic
bottles to return for cash or see the man
who every now and then walks around
naked holding a can of Ballantine Ale in
one hand and waving with the other at
uptown traffic. I plan to stop on corners
where junkies wheel and deal just to listen
to the choking songs that come out of their
strung out throats, to crack jokes with them
despite what Langston called the inner cry
tugging at our Black and Brown souls and
I will not say a word about God who knows
the politics that Easter candles cannot make
disappear. I am going to ignore the English
words that have settled in my head and listen
to some real Spanish speaking laughter that
will guide me to the biggest truths the nightly
prayers uttered by all the Saints never could
find.

THE DREAM

I dreamed of being on a bank
of the Rio Grande waiting for
nightfall, brushed by a butterfly
unburdened by borders heading
to Michoacán and her fluttering
fragile wings releasing the glory
of migrant reverie. I sat in shade
listening to the sweet songs of
grace offered by a long day, growing
older in that space and woke to the
gladness of crossing the border in
darkness. my body was bent with
prayer looking for doors to open
in heaven from which inner tubes
would drop beside me to aid the
river crossing and assure me once
in the North I would not slip into
the mouth of hell. in the river
water, I prayed a little more to
Mary's child pleading not to be
detected or blinded by tears in
the new world.

EL SALVADOR

I walked around Battery Park
searching for a postcard to send
you, the sun was out warming the
early spring morning, the vendors
had them on display and there were
kids scarred by the latest war in Europe
pointing to the Statue of Liberty in the
harbor. I could not find any postcard
to send that would speak to the bruises
you live with, the memories of the dead
and the sky that still lights up like it did
in the civil war. I woke up hearing your
tears striking the floor thousands of miles
away on the land that caresses your flesh
made from the corn we have eaten for
centuries. when I call you instead it will
be to say there were no postcards to speak
to your broken world and how glad I am
not to have mailed one with a stamp from
the country that never could hear you pray
for an end to the days on your piece of earth
disfiguring the living.

THE SERMON

we gathered to holler at the
world that cannot see white
sin, to give comfort to God's
spat on children, to talk about
Moses's Ethiopian wife and the
freedom delivered to us by the
rebel unemployed man born in
the stench of a stable to a teen
mother, unwed. we sat in old
pews left behind in the city by
people who never believed in
Brown Angels, to talk about the
day when every human being is
free and to join hands to pray for
all the people lynched in the world
after Golgotha. we stayed in that
broken down building crying out
to be woke, waiting for that damn
thing called the Holy Spirit to inject
us with the serum of truth that moves
mountains, obliterates sin and leaves
one filed with hope. we listened to the
testimony of friends who talked about
their Crucified God who crossed this
land and sat by the waters of the East
River, silent. we waited for night

just to hear heaven scream blessed are
the brutalized who shall be furnished
with light!

THE BEAUTIFUL

how beautiful is the block
when northern winds rush
through it, children play on
sidewalks, the warm rays of
the sun touches heads from
a peaceful heaven, stray dogs
are up from the alley laying
beside fire hydrants looking
like they have been granted
secret wishes and the earth's
oldest joy enfolds you. in the
kindest way the passing beauty
will endure, it will be found in
dark spaces, in a grain of sand
at Orchard Beach that reveals
the face of heaven, the gentle
smile of neighborhood widows
flexing the hold of divinity in
the world and many thin hands
lifted for prayer. how beautiful
that nothing in the city equals
the way you sit on the stoop to
imagine breathing in Spanish
speaking mountains, to set aside
the desert days, all the times of
sadness and not for a second feel
dispossessed of love.

RISE

in our divided world with
hearts breaking and filled
with fear, the time has come
to remember we are the sweet
voices to speak out, the people
not blind to justice, the restless
citizens reminiscing the wells
of democracy before which
tyrants pale. we are the people
who yet reach for the unknown,
retrace daily King's dreams and
hear the rhapsodies of heaven
burst sound into the spaces dotted
by what is now dawn's dirty light.
in choking days, we will not fold
up hope, sicken out of sight nor
sit quietly to watch the politics
at democracy's funeral. today, is
that day to rise, that time to leave
behind the crying and find again the
illustrious star that lets justice roll
like water and fills hearts with the
righteous songs of life.

THE DESK

I have the desk that sat on
a sidewalk destined for the
landfill, the one with sharp
corners the junkies on the
block breathed their colorful
words on after long tripping
nods, the one with unbalanced
draws that kept the best work
of literary aspirants who lived
on the Lower East Side, the one
I took in when a graduate student
on the same day my brother showed
up at the seminary after escaping an
apartment where occupants were shot
in a bad drug deal and the one on which
I wrote a thesis on a Reformed German
Lutheran's theology of hope admitting
God truly suffers with us. I have the desk
that survived the street, the one that has
lived with me for 42 years, the one that
reminds me of the magnificence of words,
the one with oak scars that keep me close to
it. I have the desk that has managed to
shift lives with me and that has always found
ways to feed me the English, Spanish and
Spanglish words needed to exist against
odds.

LA ISLA

the future is the blade of
grass that pushes up from
the cracks on the sidewalk
in the city that received us
after a flight from a small
island on the long gone Eastern
Airlines. we lived for years
with flowering trees and saw
mangos dangling from branches
changing colors by the day and
asking to be picked. that joy is
memory on the block, the Ponce
Social Club and the corner Bodega
where the widows gather to talk
about evenings remembered with
the sound of tiny tree frogs singing
in the distance. children grow up
on this block with stories about the
island, feeling like they want to go
there, dreaming America in Spanglish
and never turning away from the secrets
held in their mothers' hearts with pure
happiness. you can see the expectation
on the neighborhood faces, the taste of
new life on Spanish lips, and the silver
moon above rooftops cradling the Brown
kids' dreams.

WILDERNESS

I have seen the seasons
change for many years
with brighter days and
darker nights, I have
laughed with friends from
different continents, taken
flowers for others in graves
and heard birds in song
after heavy rain. I have
talked to you for months,
visited the place you left,
saw flowers opening on old
tenement fire escapes and I
cannot stop living the four
wretched hours one Easter
Sunday when saying your
name my tears fell on your
motionless body at the city
morgue. I find you now hiding
in sadness, whispering in church
and walking with those who
suffer what God at the margins
bled.

DAUGHTER

I listened to the words my
daughter hears in herself after
the highest court burning with
contradiction scrubbed out her
human rights. she is sad about
the society that offers her perfect
silence, the twisted lies justifying
the decisions of men, the power
play of Sister Amy keeping step
with the conservative Christian
legal movement that baptized her
protector of inequality. with tears
in her eyes she told me Texas is
no place for a girl to live, it does
not mix love with women's rights,
and will always put her down for
being Brown, and a girl. she
reminded me between tears
that she is today's woman being
gagged tomorrow by fools who
live in the spaces of the narrow
creeds to which she will never be
a friend. putting my arms around
her I said let's spit on this captivity
and you keep growing into that
phenomenal woman who cannot
be kept in chains.

WORD

in a country of new and
improved stupidity in which
the least competent citizens
in governance reliably reduce
the republic to a kakistocracy
of knaves, the idiots who rule,
kiss the babies and annihilate civil
and human rights have never been
happier to be followed by citizens
who pridefully wear imbecility like
a drive down a dark road without
headlights. what has driven the
nation to cheer when vulnerable
women and toddlers are assaulted
with tear cans, children are dying
in undocumented jails, Black and
Brown humanity is beaten, choked
and killed, citizens clamor for more
shock therapy instead of no guns and
women are treated to inequality by
the sanctimonious piety of those in
power full of God? in a country that
has become the standard bearer of
political stupidity and the lover of
brutalizing hate the rubbish heap
will be the last place for America
to make a stand.

ROBB ELEMENTARY SCHOOL

schools are a stage for violence,
the sound of sorrow and places
guns ring out to end forever the
days in which children play. we
watched the boys and girls lose
their innocent lives and saw their
broken bodies lowered into the
earth to become dust. the politicians
deny that spaces of education are
tax paid cemeteries that make the
broken hearted wonder seriously
about afterlife. on judgement day,
the killers with callous politicians
will cross into the land of mowed
down children and God will not
lean toward them. for now, we
all confess the news leaves us lost
for words thinking tomorrow is
another school day and kids may
return in body bags.

IRON CAGE

little sounds stitch the silence
this evening, a noisy airplane
flies high up and children's
voices play on the street with
no bursts of gunfire. why does
it feel strange to experience this
peacefulness, to see the light in
the eyes of these children tonight
not afraid of the dark, to search
for clues to their future lives in
schools and to feel myself tremble
in this moment of bitter calm? I
want to tell the people full of no
more than deadly sins that kids
in schools, churches, parks, malls
and grocery stores do not die from
love! I can hear the kids laughing
chasing each other down the street
and I question why God is so far away
in these times of sorrow and nowhere
found on earth.

THE SMALL CITY

after the little ones' flesh
turns toward the dust what is
left of them, will heavenly
gates open for them and will
Angelic voices come to earth
to offer comfort to the families
whose children were mowed down
by bullets from a demon's rifle who
obliterated every innocent dream.
yes, these beautiful lives mattered,
they had real magic in this divided
world, laughter for the sweet hours
after school and fresh sentences with
words often uttered in Spanglish that
carried mothers into the quiet hours
of night. yes, they were loved by people
striving for a better life and who have been
left with loud wailing in a near border town
of the land of the free and brave that
will hardly think twice about them. yes,
night in the small city will never end for
those exiled from light.

THE WEAK

did you ever think in these
cover up times about how the
stories of the newly arrived is
wretchedly detailed and children
head to school in fear? did you ever
think about the political sorcerers who
sell snake-oil to fools, the legislators
who trample the weak in the name
of money and the great big mound
of nonsense conspirators across the
land would have citizens believe? did
it occur to you that the blood of peasants
still wet on the streets in El Salvador
was spilled by red, white and blue paid
killers who sip wine at dinner parties
and laugh at the idea that Black lives
matter? when was the last time you
visited the cemetery where flowers
rot on the graves of those dead before
their time? someday, you will lay awake
at night to hear church bells broadcasting
the desolation and sorrow your country
offered dark-skinned human beings.

AMERICA

the beautiful things are fleshed
with thoughts beneath the stars
and the caressing air that belongs
to us. the federal politicians with
sweet rot apples on their desks can
not take them away no matter how
many ways in their private clubs they
come up with conduct to beat dark people
to their knees. the fierce affirmation of
life stands up to sing on the corners of
cities about things, irrepressible light and
ideals far from the mumbo jumbo of white
supremacists' fantasies of moral and ethnic
superiority. we are the ones who carry the
nation, the exiles, the aliens, freed slaves,
first nations, and men, women and children
with broken grammar tongues proposing a
fresh new world.

THE FLAMENCO DANCER

it never occurred to me
sitting in the circle next
to guitared Catalonian men
and my gay uncle who loved
Whitman that my mother in a
fine black dress could be so
ablaze with flamenco steps
and wood grain castanets. she
triumphantly lifted her head,
stomped her feet on the wood
floor and her tired heart poured
out of the pores of her skin like
tears. I watched recalling this
kind of dance in parts of Spain
was persecuted by law, morality
and custom long ago just like the life
this woman knew too well in the land
where white is said true. I can tell you
that magic filled the living room when
someone in the circle yelled guapa as
she lifted her dress to better slam her
heels on the floor with moves that
would have made my teachers at P.S.
66 gasp long enough to miss the holes
her steps were poking in heaven.

LATINO AT SEMINARY

in the seminary rotunda behind
a desk to receive visitors entering
the hall from windy Broadway they
come in with looks on their faces
of finding strength to believe in the
latest sediment of divinity in the
freshest theology taught. a little
ray of sunlight creaks into the space
while the sublime face of the janitor
from Guatemala smiles and shows a
gold tooth he got one migrant season
of a more youthful year. all day long
people eager to quench a thirst for
meaning enter the school believing
they will flourish in the sight of so
many fashionable religious scholars
and no one pauses to recall that the
building janitors who came from a
place pommeled by wars paid for by
citizens' taxes too are made from the
dust of the earth. the chapel adorned
with belief that does not name days of
terror or believes the cross is a lynching
tree gathers visitors in time for praise,
while Rene makes his way to trash cans
in the Quadrangle to empty them.

THE DANCE HALL

last night saturated with the
sound of salsa music, the block
smelling of sweet perfume and
chatter on the stoops shaking the
tenement windows with secrets,
we strolled to the ballroom on
Southern Boulevard for a touch
of enchantment. last night not a single
drop of rain fell in our hearts and
the wicked days that passed would
not be allowed on the dance floor. we
danced and laughed with the living
and shared more than a few steps with
the dead who visited the ballroom. we
basked in the tropical beats coming to
life in our Brown limbs and moved with
the rhythm revolting to the black tie and
patent leather shoe fake duchesses and
dukes living on the white side of town.
last night, we gathered in a noisy room
with people heaven made mending their
broken hearts in the tired city.

CAMPESINOS

have you listened to the language
of campesinos in northern towns
telling stories that blush all the
Catholic Saints, describing the
history of the bruised and poor
escaping workplace raids? have
you learned enough Spanish to
ask what it was like to walk the
desert at night with thirst, hunger,
fear and children weeping? it will
be impossible to forget them and
their underside of history lives that
were designed by decisions made in
the iconic White House never short
of bread. why don't you fill schools,
churches and the halls of Congress
with their sad tales? I do still dream
that one day you will learn to speak
campesino to cough up tears.

THE BLOOD HOURS

if we hadn't rushed into
prayer, the block would
have known a different
time, God would hurry to
bless our piece of earth
and the Boricua kids would
share their knowledge of
the world. if only we walked
a little more, followed the
light into the darkness, then
dreams would grow right for
for these colored hearts.

EL COQUI

we need more tropical sun
for the people in the barrio
worn out from work, the cold
winter months, the outraged
induced whenever white faces
say spic or when luckless kids
come home with report cards
declaring with biased letter grades
you are not good enough. we need
a religion producing sentences the
color of Spanglish, one that roams
apartments lacking multimillion dollar
Picassos on their walls and that tells
bony Puerto Rican boys and girls the
savior has the same name as Junior's
father. we need to hear more sofrito
stories from the island before everything
known about the place stolen by Uncle
Sam more than one hundred years ago is
forever lost. we need more café con leche,
frenzied dancing and the songs of tiny
tree frogs with big beautiful eyes we
call, El coqui.

DON QUIXOTE

one evening occupied by
chasing giants disguised
as windmills, when Don
Quixote began feeling old
and tired of waiting for a
countryside of windmills to
be brought to their knees by
earth rumbling beneath his
throbbing feet, with thoughts
drifting to Dulcinea who was more
beautiful than any conceivable queen,
Sancho said let me sketch your eyes
full of enchantment and thin face
delicately lined by glimmering old
and unreachable dreams: what kind
of chalk should I use?

GOOD FRIDAY

I will not spend any more time
debating the ways white collar

criminals are given a slide in the
name of political respectability.

I will not bite my tongue when
accusing you of hiding the clues

that point to the lynch rope they
purchase in a brand name store,

the medals they pin on the cops who
stomp life out of Black and Brown

lives nor naming the canonical halls
where they disrupt the good news in

defense of Good Friday. I have read
your Bible with stories that never turn

the other cheek, felt your bombs go off
in churches and wept like a throwaway

human being on this land stolen from
beloved first nations. I will tell you the

people you loath with white supremacist
ideas are strong enough to carry their

dead and they will never stop writing their
names on walls, fields, mountains, trees

and across heaven that weeps for them and
curses the plunderers who love to be seen

with bowed heads taking communion on
Sunday.

OLD BRIDGE

it was an old wood bridge with
missing planks surprising us with
a long reach across the filthy river
along whose muddy banks you could
see the tossed boot of a soldier that
once crossed it on a day expected to
be full of sin. I have seen kids from
the neighborhood train each step to
safely cross it, turning their heads back
to encourage others to follow and scaring
away birds resting on cracked railings.
looking at the old thing is enough to
frighten you and the stories told about
soldiers who tossed bodies from it in
the years of civil war will never stop
offending God.

THE RIDDLE

I was called to Washington Square
Park to read to a friend who went
blind in late life from the book by
Gabriel Garcia Marquez, *Love in
a Time of Cholera.* she loved this
story about romance that unfolded
over decades, with talk of aging, the
scent of bitter almonds, the fate of
unrequited love and the dream held
by two of winning each other back.
the love story was for her a great
companion for conversations about
the beauty of crescent moons, the
chances young lovers strolling in
the park had to find happiness and
the sound of laughter. I can tell you
she wore blindness like a magnificent
pair of pearl earrings, roamed the park
without mourning light and listened to
me read her favorite author. now and then,
I would look at her sightless brown eyes
leaning into her answer to the riddle of
love in a time of illness.

SCHOOL BOY

school boy with broken English
slowly walking to the building
where you cannot live the whole
day long, your mother just left for
work after standing for a spell to
feed you a bowl of oats where a
radio played with Spanish news
reporting most of last night's wild
mischief. school boy thinking of
the morning pledge that starts the
day, its words evacuated of rainbow
colors, your first lessons unlearning
the important places sheltering your
soul, the classrooms never noisy with
Spanish and the tempest nightmare of
being overlooked. school boy whose
mother escaped from a massacre in a
mountain village remember what the
old women said in the storefront church
hate will kill this country.

SPIC

on my way to Main Street
in the little white town, I
recall picking my Puerto
Rican hair into a perfectly
shaped natural like I was
taught on the block. my
pockets were stuffed with
unforged documents just
in case a local resident or
some curious cop decided to
stop me to say in the English
I have known since birth, go
back to your own country,
walk on your own land and
take your foreign life out of
here. I was ready each day
to listen to my country speak
to me in that little Ohio town
about how offensive it found
my Afro-Puerto Rican hair in
its world of blissful ignorance
about God's own very diverse
earth. sometimes, on late night
walks with tears rolling down
my face, I would raise fists to
heaven demanding to know why

people in that Midwest town and
and even college educators never
found me human like them. lately,
the college sends me fund raising
letters in the naked language of the
inclusivity it never gave and with
my Spanglish tongue I imagine the
place still believes I am nothing more
than a trash spic.

THE BLAST

ears in the world have
caught news of threats

to Ukraine about bursting
light that makes thousands

vanish and places in the way
no more than cindering bits

of rubble. together, we are
living time before the great

destruction and the love story
about God that itself has been

passed along in the adored
good book in many languages

too will be turned by a tyrant
into ashes. the widows in the

borderland nation pray for the
radioactive murderer, the grand

friend of oblivion, not to make
landfall on them in the name of

the Kremlin's peace that kills
ethically innocent human beings.

the world is watching the killing
game of an arrogant old man, the

seasoned killer from a lost past,
eager to show us there will be no

war once he annihilates a nation
that is standing in the way of his

deranged quest to renew Russia. we
are weeping now without tears and

are no less appalled by Russian
threats of nuclear fire than not

being able to look directly into
the eyes of God to say stop the

madness made by the flaws in
your potter's hands.

THE SHADOWS

the fallen will not
grow old with the

changing seasons
in Ukraine but we

will mourn and pray
for them, remember

the names of mothers
with children flattened

by bombs and the citizens
who died for the cause of

freedom. in the sad sky
over Kyiv the earth holds

the ashes of those who
have gone on their way

and the living bite their
lips cursing the enemy

turning streets red and
remaking with mourning

and pain the souls Putin
slices up in the name of

his upside-down world.
those who are dying on

the other side of the world,
the human flesh that mirrors

the divine, are God's children
senselessly killed by a tyrant

that will never escape penance
nor shame. from sunrise to

nightfall. he will hear the voices
of the slain in the wind, spoken

by trees, stones, rubble, ruins
and ashes. and the Ukraine refugees

will say that what remains amid
the cruel losses is freedom, and

life.

THE WAR

I remember the days of war
in a tiny country most of the
world never heard named, the
frightening screams of children
who ran away from soldiers, and
the thought that this is exactly
how human flesh is turned to blood
and ashes. today, tanks fire on
Ukrainian kindergarten classes under
orders from covetous old men who no
longer confess God created us for
each other. I recall Salvadoran soldiers
who slaughtered everything in their
path, a teacher from a community
where I broke bread with the poor
who was decapitated for loving those
who spoke against a military regime,
priests we buried, nuns raped unto
death and wounded campesinos begging
for miracles to rain from heaven. now,
I cannot stand the long speeches of a
Russian tyrant, the cheapening of the
life of terrorized people and once again
the criminal violence of war.

MORNING

when sitting alone beside
the splashing river in this
world older than written
history, enchanted by the
words in the Bible passed down
before English, absorbed by the
mysteries of creation, the divine
made flesh, the prayers spoken
alone, I do pay attention to the
tender shadows making peace
with all things. I hear a hammering
woodpecker, experience the blues
retreating with morning light and
I am still enough to say Lord keep
me.

SCHOOL ASSEMBLY

the Irish-American music teacher
raised his baton to begin the public
school assembly concert with his
latest students who looked on with
wide-eyes. the woodwind and brass
players unsure about fingering stared
like they hoped the walls of Jericho
would come down and maybe a tiny
salsa beat or two. the music class at
the beginning of the year started with
a single note the conductor insisted required
feeling though for the dark boys and girls
in the room less privileged by the color
of their skin moods were composed with
tropical beats, spiritual blues and sounds
passed along by people less free. you see,
these kids were used to walking passed the
locked doors of the church and beyond the
corner where junkies shouted in harmony
dope, smack, scar, chiba, tecata, chicle,
tigre del norte and meth. these kids familiar
with a howling world who always gave a
a priceless performance knew concert A
and every note hanging on trees in their
imagined Eden.

SILENCE

I am sitting beside the bed of a
friend slowly drifting into the
final hour, words never more
clear, doubts arising to be taken
away by a gentle breeze and an
illness that does not fall behind
in its work. we share memories,
talk around the fear of what cannot
be undone and I look into his eyes
full of life telling everyone in the
room existence matters in ways not
familiar until the end. no one expected
he would be unable to stand in the
yard beneath the tree that has not lost
all her leaves. no one expected to see
his cherished wife feeding him peaches,
while whispering curses to the gods that
did not listen to prayers for just a little
bit more of the world. God will not hold
it against us to pray for a miracle, keep
company with this ill man into the last
night or for believing when silence finally
arrives this ill soul will surely know better
than any of us the love that comes from on
high.

THE SACRIFICE

they walked a long way
on their knees to the altar
of the church high up a hill
with repentance secreted
by sorry flesh. these women
looked like the old beggar
who has sat on the cathedral
steps and slept on them under
sacks for more years than the
local priests recalled. the wind
let loose unkind words hollered
by the perverts of violence to the
women taking steps on their knees
more numerous than the village
missing and dead. I witnessed the
procession disclosing some kind of
truth like a lifted veil, observing the
brave women of God declare their
place in the world and with every
step leaving in it a presence full of
fight. they see life differently and I
suspect not a single Pharaonic chariot
could ever stop them from making
their pious trek on these primeval
streets.

HOSPITAL

in the middle of the night the
emergency room is crowded
with overdosed addicts, old
men in business suits unable
to stand straight with blood
stains on white shirts, hookers
in a corner rubbing their thighs
and looking with suspicion at
who will be examined first and
children crying. in a corner of
the waiting room a flat screen
T.V. flashes yesterday's breaking
news, the night nurse calls out
names and a priest from St. Rita's
church around the corner rushes
into a room to offer prayer to the
teen junkie shot on Avenue B who
can't stop yelling Father stop the
bullshit. a few more people enter
the waiting room, the women with
braided hair from Michoacan who
sells tamales on Houston Street is
half-asleep with her left arm in a
sling, the room is noisy with the
sounds of different tongues saying
no one will be put together fully
the same.

IMPERFECT EDEN

one morning in the ruins
of a slum crowded with
worn out lives, old world
souls voiced Spanish hymns
in a storefront church, factory
workers felt sentimental for
days cutting sugarcane, elderly
men read letters on a stoop from
other lives and people on the
tired block free fell into a dark
paradise. the priest who liked
to drink beer at church street
fairs, the one that never met an
Angel, forgave petty theft, knew
too little about love and hate walked
the sidewalk unable to name even one
stammering tongue neighbor. he looked
around helplessly, mostly upset with the
scuff on his new black shoes calmly
believing his good book contained a
theory of life for the poor whose lives
had been damned for centuries by
Empires.

STRANGE

strange how stray dogs
on the block are in the
alley on their knees with
tongues sagging like an
afternoon plea. strange
how widows stroll home
together from church after
collecting a little joy and
feeling a chill of hope in
a dark place. strange how
the Lord in heaven has not
sent us news for so long
down here.

DARK WORDS

there are words for darkness
I can only say in Spanish, they
keep track of the junkies on the
block, the light almost visible
when old women make the sign
of the cross, or whenever I say
the names written on the alley
wall off Avenue D that no white
eyes have ever seen. the dark
makes me feel lonely, further
from the lights in the old building
windows and estranged from the
promises of a divine being. I recall
an evening walking with my father
to Simpson Street, seeing hookers
sitting on the bottom step of the
Subway Station massaging tired
feet inside of thick stockings and
smiling at me, the smell of fresh
pizza picked up for a meal and
wanting to invite little Rosa who
was out hustling to come for a slice.
I hear Spanish church songs trying
to disable the darkness and think the
sadness down here is on its way to
a God of change.

CREATION

another year has passed
with God too abstractly
present in the rude hours
of hurled stones. people
kneel before altars and
on the sporting fields to
wait for a divine being to
speak just a few words in
any language, to break the
silence and wash the world
that thinks it is enough to
confess, clean. in the year
of happenings, this time in
which money takes priority
on justice scales, this time
defined by the slithering impact
of pious hate and the incessant
blathering of stupid politicians,
we wonder on bruised knees is it true
you God made us for better things?
you see, these last few years has
made it hard to believe you created
us from the earth and called the work
good.

GRADUATION

today like no other was made
for stepping slowly over the lines
on God's earth, to throw open the
doors of wonder and let the caged
birds go free. today the ticking clock
was like a dream within a dream not
confident of keeping time inside of us,
lacking a single bell to loudly toll as
joy touched us. today you are telling
stories of the road taken, the one only
a few pointed out to you, the path that
in an age of illness suggested even hope
was grim. today, you with friends who
wore the same don't give up smile stay
close to not stumble. Today, the patched
up fragments of hope paraded in many
colors in front of watchful eyes here and
on a screen across the border, family listened
to your name called out on a stage for you
to receive a college diploma. today, family
in two countries breathed graduation like
incense in Mass.

STAY WOKE

truth is dead in this country
that rejects facts quicker than
freedom of speech. book bans on
authors of color define the latest
delusional racial panic from citizens
fearful about people with dark skin,
while their violent white mobs refuse
being woke. moral indigestion sets in
when school kids are kept from reading
Rudolfo Anaya, Toni Morrison, Alice
Walker, Isabel Allende, Grace Lin, James
Baldwin, Jill Twiss, Sherman Alexie or
E.L. James for pity's sake. one can only
wonder why citizens believe speeches
declaring its fine to teach history wrongly
and praise vicious bigots. telling lies will
not keep education true and white racist
history kicked out of public school is just
another rope neck tie for dark necks crying
out freedom is still wrecked.

THE HANGING TREE

while you dance around that
burning cross, you think night
will not ever swallow up the
world of your making to shatter
your invented superior worth? you
think the murdered dark children
of the nation will finally keep quiet
and rocks from heaven will not drop
on your vacuous heads? you think
sacred Black and Brown feet will
refrain from walking all over you
on the way to the promised land?
when the sun rises smiling, you will
understand justice belongs to those
who follow a lynched, dark-skinned
savior.

SPANISH HARLEM

the writing on the steps
of Spanish Harlem is unlike
University English that drifts
in like the fog that carried slave
traders to this shore. the writing
on the stoops in the land of the
beautiful is scripted with the
language that keeps alive illegal
dreams, fights with Devils that
won't let go and young high school
graduates who give up college
dreams. let me translate the words
on the steps of the building on the
corner of Third Street and Avenue
D stretching beyond themselves to
lean into a rattled world, each one
registering Brown lives in elapsed
time, written by people carrying the
city and Cathedrals on their backs
and more familiar with still life than
a Cèzanne painting. let me share just
a few stories about Carmen Julia who
did not make it to sweet sixteen or
Wilfredo who dropped out of middle
school to lastly rest eternally in an
underground hole or the kid whose

name is on the steps—Jose—who
graduated from Cooper Union two days
before his brother died of an OD on a
rooftop. in Spanish Harlem English
words you see are not enough to account
for the lives that cough out such blistering
days.

ANNO DOMINI

the new year is already
inviting me to have blind
faith in new life, to let the
paid theologians ask about
the existence of God, not
see grey clouds covering
light, dispatch flowers to
graves and listen closely to
songs inspired by the very
first manger. to tell the truth, I
expect God not to live elsewhere
next year, to find time to talk at
length to poor single mothers,
border crossing refugees and
homeless migrant kids. in the
new year, I would like to hear
less about the purity and gentleness
of the first-century Jew lynched on
a tree and notice more confessional
types with hearts to feel and sorrow
in their eyes finding the dark colored
Galilean in brothers and sisters of the
same hue who never hesitate to take
a stand against hate, the opiate church
and the instinct to save oneself. in the
coming days, I hope we can love God

in the very flesh sacred literature says
is varied and good.

RING-A-LING

by golly the pandemic has
skipped by the halls decked
with holly to steer the season
away from the silver bells,
the magic and the wonder of
the birth of Jesus in that old
smelly stable. soon, it will
be Christmas Day though the
noises of holiday cheer are not
audible in varied places. perhaps,
in this year of illness, it is the sound
of each other's voices that matter,
the simple touch of a hand, or being
in the same room with family and
friends drawing in the air like an
unwrapped gift. perhaps, the last
three limping years has left us all
feeling too weary to deck the halls
with cheer but I give thanks yet for
the Christmas story and the thought
no one now disagrees with the Grinch
that Christmas does not come from a
store, the lights, the trees, but the great
spirit of peace.

ETERNAL SPRING

they are weeping today on
Avenue D with eyes more
ancient than the city named
for a Duke and the innocent
tears are drenching sidewalks.
they are lighting God's candles
in front of the building on the
West Side of the little bridge
leading to the East River and
burning newspapers in a trash
can that impersonate stories
about truth. they are beginning
to load the night into an uptown
bus to travel with undocumented
exiles and I am not there to see
the Brown faces smiling light.
they will not name the country with
their Spanish speaking mouths, speak
of its razor-sharp violence, hateful
insults or churchy promises. they
will whisper to each the contents of
their aching hearts to reveal what led
them North to experience a new world
paradise.

EASTER NIGHT

I saw my brother walking
in a dream last night on Walton
Avenue. there was a high
tolling bell escaping from
an apartment window out
of which an old woman with
soft eyes looked at Rudy who
was laughing out loud leading
a line of friends who having left
this world before their time were
not complaining. I saw children
examining Easter decorations on
apartment windows unaware the world
would not offer a single penny to save
them, time to wail for them or an amen
to honor their Spanish names. I saw
Rudy dead on the sidewalk named by
the block junkies of the street that fears
no cops. there was no crowd around him,
no ambulance, no lover, no friends, no
priest. I wept in the dream before the
emptiness that greeted my junkie brother,
raised my fist at heaven for not hearing
prayers, tore out my heart thinking this
is the history of my people and thanked
the cop who opened the pocket Bible Rudy

carried with my telephone number on a scrap
of paper in it that read, brother. I woke up
hearing an Easter hymn coming from another
apartment and wondered if some Angel had
carried my brother to a place abundant
with milk and honey.

THE RIVER

this is the little creek with a
patch of trees at a distance
from the apartments visited
nightly by the president's men
in search of Beto who has worked
for the last eight years washing
dishes. at the edge night, his son
walks to the Bronx River hiding
in the hallway from the government
thugs. Shorty's friends would meet
him at the water front from which fishing
boats sailed daily in time to catch the
rising sun from a quiet spot on the aging
sea. by the time Shorty arrived at the
swimming hole several of his school mates
were already dripping wet, the sound of
Willie Colon was threading from an old
radio inspiring kids to dance on a rusting
train bridge that carried white middle-class
workers from suburbs to jobs in the city.
the friends Shorty met at their private beach
talked in perfect English, traced memories
in the only country they had ever known and
saturated the East River banks with the stories
the regime thugs denied.

FAMILIA

family, on this circling
earth the Angels will
think back about the
many ways you helped
me hang love in my
heart. I confess with you
each wound is bathed
with light, the shadows of
different times pushed out
to sea and the kind gift of
splendid life, mine!

NEW YEAR

what can be said of the
passing year? well, when
midnight drifted into us
an old year with dazzling
joys and glorious pains
turned another page. today,
we give prayer for a world
in sickness and forgiveness
to those who hate us. in the
new beginning, let us bundle
mercies from above, thicken
the meaning of love and stand
like faithful messengers of God
against madness. today, let us
walk, run, stumble, and crawl
into magnificent new times.

THE RENT

the rent is harder to
make than heaven and
the music upstairs still
sounding out from vinyl
needled on Emilia's old
radiola does not cost a
penny. the love songs
wail and when the salsa
plays we dance without
a dime to our names until
forever that comes next
week. we can't move to the
building across the street
or three blocks away you
see for the landlord is still
going to bother us and we
won't stop being broke and
for damn sure the church
raffle will not keep us from
petty theft for a little cash to
make ends meet and keep from
living on the streets.

LIGHT FROM DARKNESS

we been going to church
since our mothers walked
in them to find rest, water
was placed on our heads, and
tired men and women with dark
skin needed to say prayers in a
place unlike the centers of bent
over of work. we been kneeling
with thankful hearts in the only
home that never called us filthy
poor, illegal aliens and good for
nothing spics. we been singing
like kids in this space called church,
full of hope and missing whips to
scar us permanently with grief. we
been talking out loud in Spanish on
the church steps grateful to be blessed
by the God of Moses who understands
slaves and promises that water will rush
out of the wilderness and streams reach
us on parched earth. we been sitting here
after lighting candles to Mother Mary,
listening to the blowing wind and in low
voices confessing to each other that in
this tiny piece of paradise we know how
to live unbroken!

AGING

he sits on a park bench with
a battered book read for a third
time recalling his first days of
school after a long summer in
the city. the people known to
him for many years are passing
away, some unable to remember
their names, others cared for by
hired help and the numbers that
were carefully stored in a smart
phone are revised by the week
it seems. a few old men stroll in the
local park not giving up to chronic
conditions and the widows always
in black walk by the bodega recalling
every love and loss in their lives that
still grow deeper. he notes the drifting
clouds, the White Throated sparrows,
the children at play seeing the things
he has long forgotten and oddly in his
mind erupts an old delicious love poem
learned by heart. yes, he has aged like
others though with a wrinkled hand time
still holds him up for a little more to see
and feel in plain time.

SPANGLISH

when I was asked where does
Spanglish come from I answered
it is beaten out on congas from
park benches across the city, it is
pushed into space by the stormy
voices of Ricans living on the Lower
East Side, it originates with shouting
children at play in the dark alleys
of the barrio and it shows up with
beautiful mixed tongues from noisy
streets. it is speech translated from
the words of young mothers who
say mijito in the morning before kids
head to rebel in public school, it is the
roar of the tropical ocean making an
appearance on the Long Island Sound,
the look in abuela's eyes after she kisses
Jesus on the cross attached to the rosary
that came with her from a Spanish world
and it is the wrinkled hands that have
known too many days of back breaking
work. Spanglish comes from the soul of
hungry people with no tears left to weep
in their world rich with dreams.

SACRED MOTHER

Maria del Carmen, sweet Mother of
Jesus, known by many other names,

but always a mother to our dark brother
called from Galilee. I have been writing

letters to you since the third grade when
I discovered an image of you standing

behind a flame dancing on the wick of
a candle picked up in the Perez bodega

on Intervale Avenue. You may remember
the first words I shared were that we exist

in the Bronx too poor to bring you anything
valuable at the local church save the look

in the eyes on top of thin bodies asking for
no more than a simple hug. Sagrada Madre,

do you remember the warmth of my hands
the day I joined a group of women in church

who were dusting Saints, the Spanglish prayer
I scattered on the altar from which you observed

things and the love I promised was yours forever
to keep? Perhaps, in one of your manifestations

you are aware that we have been dying on these
streets where the cops drive by in brand new cars

laughing, the kids going to public school spend
time trying to figure out how to break away from

lessons teaching them to be even more invisible,
and in churches in which messages ask us to forget

the Puerto Rican blood no one denies wanders in
our veins. Virgen del Carmen, Guadalupe, Cobre,

y la Paz I am placing a bouquet of flowers on the
altar today not to bribe you or anything but I do

hope you send a sign to let us all know that you
hear the voices lifting songs to you and know the

feelings of rebellion lingering in the hearts
hiding beneath brown skin in a world too familiar

with Dante's hell.

THE HOUSE

the house you bring
across three borders
pushed into a tiny black
backpack is a space of
mango trees, café served
in the middle of day with
buttered bread bought from
the kid selling it from his
bicycle and dinner with a
mother who never wished
to see you leave. you carry
it wherever you go untying
memories from it, letting the
children who played in front
of the dwelling laugh these days
in the living room of your English
world flat, recalling with things
you carefully grasp in the bag like
the smell of freshly peeled oranges
in a tropical wind, the barking
dogs in the colonia and chatter
from all around in search of some
peace. two nights ago, I saw you
reach in the bag to open the door
of a room where a candle burns on
top of a note that says or so you

told me it is hard to live in a North
country between God and the devil
too happy making bets about us.

DOPE FIENDS

there was an apartment
on Longfellow Avenue
with no furniture save a
mattress in what passed
for a bedroom. that place
never experienced a lick
of time with care and the
door leading into the space
had a hole where a lock had
been for many years. it was
always dark inside though at
night candles could be seen
through the hole in the door
illuminating a table on which
junkies stored illicit treasures
for those who came by with
cash for dope. exchanges were
made through the mouth on the
door that carried with a breeze the
smell of King Pine to remind the
junkies they were dirty. every day
we came early to knock on the door,
set life to the side, collect glassine
bags without a single flower and rush
to rooftops where the newly dead from
an OD had been removed to stick needles

into veins like writers once dipped pens into
inkwells to save the world from monsters
with strange words. I can tell you we became
experts by age eleven at finding veins in this
country going out of its way to smother us.

TALK

let's talk about the joyful revelations
you find on the stoop of a tenement
that is always full of music and love
from across the border. let us dream
of being somewhere else, in the place
we call our own country and is a skip
over the ocean to what has been an island
colonized by Uncle Sam. let us recall
grimy corners on the block where we
gathered with others to talk Spanglish
about being born in a city hospital
called the butcher shop. let us talk about
things that matter, the hope we find in
living and that moves in us like rushing
water from the East River. let us talk about
the children of a world more ancient than
this English city that is part of a republic
that builds Walls on the border and nails
doors shut.

THE BUS

the bus is noisy with
crying children, voices
speaking in the name of
the frail and loud beating
from sluggish hearts that
dream of a world full of
things set right. a mother
with an infant in her arms
bounces on the back wheel,
the ages roll backwards out
the bus windows and a girl
with long dark hair slides
one open to spit. moving
lights on the road compete
with the darkness, the rabbit
foot on the drivers rear view
mirror knocks about with the
bumps on the road unable to
keep still. the sun falls behind
mountains and the elderly
couple that boarded the bus in
Guatemala is debating how long
until they reach their stop. the
bus loaded with friends, family
and strangers pushes its way to
the border speaking Spanish with

voices border guards will deduce
come from nowhere.

GOD

I knocked on your door
yesterday expecting the
thin barrier to open to let
me have a view of your
heavenly mansion. you did
not answer the knock then but
I shared words with the dreams
of others at your place. you know
better than anyone my ways of
seeing you leaning over the barrio
from heaven are unlike those of
Roman collared priests or Pentecostal
Preachers who promise to free souls
and have not yet managed to keep
poor kids alive. I wonder are you
in the wind that makes us laugh,
the waves rushing to the banks at
Orchard Beach, the pigeons flown
on Shorty's roof that tumble in flight
making the Puerto Rican girls scream,
or a secret message carried by bird
songs for the us? last night, I saw a
falling star skipping through the night
sky and thought you decided to make an
appearance to put an end to back breaking
days mocking you on earth.

BROKEN STEPS

I have been sitting on the
broken steps for several hours
seeing the elderly who once
belonged in Puerto Rico walk
down Avenue D. this is when
I would love to have a suitcase
full of ripe mangos to peel open
with loving fingers to offer them
and then invite their stories on the
stoop to untie the knots that keep
us awake at night. I hear voices
racing up the street, waking the
silence, sweeping over the sidewalks
with words drawn from hymns known
to block pietists and finally landing on
my Spanglish lips. I look around these
American streets like a rejected guest
and huddle with the homeless and the
foreigners that are busy remapping in
their heads the borders that kill widows,
orphans and the poor. on the broken
steps, among nameless people who die
hungry I ask what truth in this country
is self-evident?

ABANDONED

someday they will weep
for you under the moon light
like you leaked for your sister
in the slant shade of a Bronx
cemetery. someday they will
look at your Brown face to see
the soft hand of God that made
it and they will curse the world
that feared your color. someday,
they will look upon your misery,
see your hard-working kin, hear
the stories of frantic flight, notice
the days of graveyard sadness and
they will cry with you. someday,
you will recall stories of the slave
ships, the violence of empire, the
gun report on the streets, the jail
cell on Rikers Island, the cop's baton
that made you bleed, and mourning
apartments. someday, a band of Angels
will come to the rescue and you will
be lifted by them to heaven.

WINTER

it was quiet after
the snowstorm and
we laid in the flakes
listening for the cracking
ice that speaks to God
for us. the voices of the
children that weathered
the storm chased each
other into the warmth
of a fire inside, where
crackling wood made
us feel in chilling bones
the truest mysteries of
love that long ago fell
from heaven.

UNDOCUMENTED

you will wake up with
yesterday's sadness and
the same illegal label. you
will work five days and get
paid for three and feel caged
in the country that jingles
hate. you will call across
the border to get news and
bear the weight of this city
on the tip of the broom handed
to you by a white man with a
tan. you will speak in a language
America calls tongues, feel like a
hostage kneeling before the barrel
of a gun and look into blue eyes on
long subway rides. you will wake
up today in a single room sighing
about life, then spend the rest of the
time cleaning toilets for the white
man.

THE BISHOP

in the tiny Lutheran church
whose cross was arrested by
soldiers who judged it subversive
material the bishop says prayers
for those living in dim light. the
screams of his broken world were
heard around the world when the
soldiers got to firing and every
sign of weakness in him pointed
to God's own strength against the
savage State and its multinational
crooks.

THE VILLAGE

again, I walked the villages
where leaving comes with a

great cost to the mothers who
hold infants in their arms, toss

bread to the birds that live close
to them and stories are still shared

about the missing. I visited an old
church with many years evident by

the faded paint and a priest born in
an indigenous hamlet miles away

leads it like he always belonged in
this Colonia. I found him with the

widows who come to dust the Saints
musing about the world weeping and

talking about people wearing twisted
thorns around their heads. everything

that ever happened to the poor lurks
in the neighborhood and Father Ulysses

stays up nights trying to figure out a
thousand ways to relieve the pain. there

are still youth coming to Mass though
fewer are seen walking the unlabeled

streets and if you listen closely to what
is said many have fled the savagery of

a broken country for the unfriendly cities
North of here. they will work to the bone

for the petty wages of exile and minus
aid from heaven will send a few dollars

home for others to eat. kneeling, I
pray for the precious Lord to pull

them by hand to a new Eden!

DREAMERS

someone was talking about
the skipping children in front
of the bodega where old men
play dominoes and read news
printed in el diario la prensa,
while rappers keep it real and
bachata plays from a second
story window. lovers, junkies,
hustlers, street-walkers and the
story-tellers are sitting with us
on the stoop loving life in this
beat up barrio like this stretch
of the city was paradise and her
people are teaching the whole
damn east village to sing lelolai
in pitch. someone noticed the
bus heading North on Avenue
D, exiled Central Americans
basking on fire escapes with
Butchy yelling for Rafi to come
hang with the Boricuas sucking
up warm air. someone said we
are Black and Brown people in
a country stomping dreams.

EMMAUS

on the road a stranger
startled them with truth
about the lynching outside
the city gates and the coming
of heaven down to earth. they
felt longing in their hearts, the
shocking sadness and despair for
the one no longer with them. they
listened to the man masquerading
as a stranger who walked beside
them and in broken hearts recalled
the night they left Jesus alone in a
place visited by thugs with clubs.
on the long walk they thought hope
ended on a cross and it was pointless
any longer to believe. the stranger on
the road to Emmaus, after conversation
on the road, sat with them for a quiet
meal and with rough carpenter hands
offered them life again from broken
bread in the name of the cause never lost
and for the sake of everything made for
touch and taste.

THE WIDOW

when the streetlights come
on at night, the stray dogs
that rummage trash lay down,
the tenement windows show faint
images of the elderly looking out
at the evening and kids on the
block play their last game of round
up tag, that is when you get a peek
at life on the block. you may not be
up to reading the signs that would
easily fill the pages of several books,
or make out the grammar of Spanglish
sentences uttered on the stoop. I can
tell though when Hector conjures evening
prayer at his storefront church and the
junkies on the corner tease the little kids,
you see Mother Mary dressed in a black
dress walking along Avenue D and by
the wall with the name of her dead
husband.

THE WALK

we walked the streets of
a massacred village reading
lament into what was left
of the burned down church,
the grove of bushes that hid
a woman with paradise's keys
in her broken heart. I listened
to you sigh on a cracked bench
disbelief for the crime against
the simple poor committed by
soldiers, tears pouring down
like prayers for El Mozote. we
heard tragic stories, viewed the
darkness in divine light, paused to
mourn with the village women
testifying about the weight of the
Cross planted in that fresh site
of Calvary. I remember sharing
the cries of the wounded, praying
for the dead and breaking bread in
Spanish with peasants that refused
to drip fear. I can still see you the
military chaplain who cursed that
upside-down world that took the life
of the innocent and received blessings
even from the departed for speaking truth

and condemning a world that kills in the
name of God.

THE SUBWAY RIDE

on the subway ride with
rain pouring on the streets
above ground, a woman with
a gracious voice enters the car
to sing, a teen who loves the
melody joins in, an elderly man
looking eager to tell Yeats smiles
looks at the vocalist. the sound of
joy fills the subway car, riders forget
the rain outside and they appear to
imagine warmer days when coats are
shed. the passengers going places felt
free to overdose on the idea of falling
blindly in love with someone. two Mexican
newcomers speaking Spanish whisper
something about the dark tunnel and
memories of their native land. They are
not treated like strangers on the subway
and there is difference in their fare for
the underground ride.

WALK TO GOLGOTHA

after Christ was killed,
the little village left in
flames, houses were
delivered to ruin and
stones were placed to
cover the church yard
graves, people who could
fled. they learned prayers
required for escape, recalled
what they meant to say in
the placita to the priest who
came to say goodbye and
give them one more look
at his messenger of God
face. Mothers with kids
who knew paradise was lost
planned to run North with
the wind and try their fate
with other gods that perhaps
dared not say to them you are
nothing. they fled the days of
harvesting fields to the perils of
pushing mops, nannying white
children and living with their
precious own in a rented back
room, midway to nowhere. they

planned to spend hard-earned days
praying for a little light to shine on
their kids growing up in Spanglish
in a foreign world.

STREET KIDS

I looked at the clouds
sobbing last night for the
children living on these
streets forgotten a little
more each day. they sat
on the abandoned building
steps with disturbed faces
muttering to each other
while the dark night spread
across the block. I could see
they would love to go back
to that place they once called
home, look out an apartment
window and imagine childhood
dreams, again. they have already
stopped talking about heavenly
things and messages from a
God who never thinks of them.
these kids are the disappeared,
kidnapped, tortured, locked in
jail or those killed. they are the
innocent flesh never thought of
who die on the streets.

THE GAZE

people who never set foot
in the barrio world shoot
their cold-blooded hate at
the beautiful Black night
and earth Brown faces that
hold truth in their eyes and
the soul breaking lies of a
twisted nation. we are the
fallen pieces of the night sky,
the dust of God's brown earth,
the blood spilled for centuries
by the enslaved, exploited, beaten,
hanged and burned. we are the
brothers and sisters of a Crucified
Jew, every voice you won't lift, the
people with the stranger names you
never bother to say, the beautiful
dark boys and girls on the sidewalks
at play while gospel choirs sing. how
can you imagine a multicolored world
reduced to whiteness? believe me
heaven hears us snapping the chains
made by your sick vision of the USA.

GOVERNOR

dear governor shooting
transgendered youth full of
defiling words, exercising
the bully mechanisms of
hate, denying the evidence
of diversity on God's good
earth, parading in public with
a demonizing attorney general
who reeks of criminality, stop
choking the work of heaven on
earth. the trans-youth you deny civil
rights, the human beings you find
unworthy of love, kids subjected
to abuse, terror, suffering and hate
are Mister governor going to outlive
you and they will always be more
precious than your mockery of the
law!

HOPE

hope rises in the morning
in the kitchen still carrying
sleep, it pours into you like
coffee that lifts your feet,
it listens to mysteries not
solved, delivers you to the
side of the meek to hold up
the sky once again with a
single hand. hope is a shy
friend in the dark, a balm
giver for sad times, a thing
near but often unseen. hope
is a playground of speech,
a mover of mountains and
a teller of truth. hope is a
thing that shouts be not afraid
you shall overcome if not now
then someday.

BEGGAR

the old man has pushed that
grocery cart down Avenue D
since the bodegas popped up
on the corners all the way to
fourteenth street. he carries
a purse full of change made
from selling bottles and cans
he collects all day when not
slumped against the building
across from the projects he
lived as a kid. sometimes, he
pushes the cart to stand by the
entrance to the subway station
next to Cooper Union and begs
students to spare some change
like a shepherd on a hillside
searching for lost sheep. now
and then someone asks for his
name, listens to him tell stories
about the reaper who roams the
East River Park and imaginative
tales about Angels with flawed
words making promises about
the renewal of life and a great
banquet in a place too far from
his inflamed streets. when he's

done with all the once upon a
time bulletins, he pushes that
cart through bumper to bumper
cars back to Avenue D like an
ageing man who hiked an arid
desert back to an Oasis that has
a bodega to offer him a can of
Ballantine beer. at night, he
rests on a bench on the walkway
beside the river with the moon
escorting him into a world full of
tropical dreams.

PEACE

the news speeds across the
airways, the images appear
on social media, the pictures
of war crimes, the victims,
the lovers of freedom and
murder filling our eyes like
the blood of Ukraine that
is splattered by the second
on crumbling walls. the verdict
of the world is on the head
of the man who cut his teeth
with the KGB and the nauseating
truth of children, men and women
dead leaves a rabid record of Good
Friday. there are those in my country
who curl up to view massacres for their
delight, yet many others only hear the
cries of those who suffer and then they
pray to the God who sides with victims
for peace.

NEW TESTAMENT

I have not stepped into the
cold church to hear a preacher
with empty words. I am never
missed by the people who have
never seen shooting galleries or
talked to kids with abscesses tracing
their names on bony arms. these
days I kneel on the rooftops
tossing curses to heaven while
staring up at the sky more certain
God will not reply. I have been
to the Cathedral on Fifth Avenue
since Lefty died on Simpson
Street, alone. You know how
difficult it is to see images of
the Holy family and frescoes
of white suffering on the walls
and not a single dark-skinned
human being imaged in these
fancy sanctuaries. in my something
else world the junkie children say
we were the first people to walk
in God's Garden then after the fall
rejected by Adam and Eve, we were
enslaved, beaten, lynched and kept
out of choice seats in soiled houses
of worship.

KINDNESS

kindness is unknown
until you live for others,
experience life like an
autumn leaf floating to
the earth and you deposit
the prejudice and shadows
you dare not speak in the
world of no return. you
must travel roads seldom
taken, see the people left
for dead on the curb and
weep with the moist tears
of children and victims
of war. kindness must be more
honest than sermons about
love and prayers for a world
only longing for peace.

RICHES

it's hard to remember why
people said that in America
streets are paved with gold
and life is monstrously easy.
you see, when the young men
gathered beneath the old Ceiba
tree they believed it would only
take a little time to rise up the
northern class ladders. they really
had no idea it meant coughing up
work place dust, butchery house
plumage and plain old Spanish
curses. it's hard not to think this
country with its religious heresies,
villages and farms will sit to weep
with us by the waters of Babylon. it's
hard to hear the poor hemorrhaging on
the block talk about foreign villages
soaked in blood and my country spitting
on people with dark skin and dirt beneath
their nails.

SOCCER HILL

what is the meaning of a day
in the life of the kids playing
soccer on a mountain top packed
with glorious mystery? how
often will you look into their
Brown smiling faces trembling
and wordless for that remarkable
moment? I confess children are
worldly maps leading to heaven, the
face of places worth visiting and the
innocent flesh of life! today, on this
hilltop, watching the simplicity of a
game on an improvised field, no one
dares believe the broken world is
hopeless.

COLDER VOICES

we have been sitting on
the stoop for most of the
morning with the Spring
sky watching over us like
it has in public for those
who walked to the border
expecting to be saved by
a Christian nation. those of
us with family who made
it across are anxious to know
about the lands once called
home and we look at each
other aware of not yet being
free in self-congratulating
America. life is very odd
where you are not wanted,
poverty is gift wrapped for
you and God is a pale faced
loathing mute who blesses the
rich. little Tito who claims he
reads the future in Spanglish
hands says even the churches
close the door, people inside
are shouting I told you not to
come but the barrio will keep
giving us lavishly colorful

flowers. it's funny how sitting
on the stoop adjusts your mind
to beautiful dark kin questioning
the white theology that finds too
many ways to ignore the truth
of a Crucified God.

TOGETHER

on the hill beneath a cloudy
sky with the moon drifting
steadily away from this place
a hummingbird flashed into
foggy silence. we moved to
the long table grasped then by
the ecstatic spirits of ancient
lands pushed into prayer by the
memories of the weeping souls
who crossed boundaries to talk
to us of their sorrowing hearts
and warmest hope. we heard
the ghastly stories, walked the
bloody stained earth, recalled
with the poor the devastation
of those who dared defend them
against the furies of the rich and
compliant State. we paused in
the channels of time reveling in
the beauty of the landscape and
reached with this people of corn
into the world before creation in
which the woes too familiar to the
wretched of the earth, end.

THE LIMIT

I reached the very limit
of prayer in this country
that hardly recognizes the
wonders in elegant dark
faces and Spanglish tongues.
I will talk true to the authors
in high places allowed the
authority to instruct readers
about how to think about the
barrios they rarely visit. I have
witnessed too many years of
Black and Brown lives held up
by shape-shifting academics,
ethicists and crazed theologians
dishonestly teach lessons about
us and say ghastly things. I have
reached the end of a long train
ride into the privileged neighborhoods
of a nation with many white fragility
scholars teaching in a book banning
society other pale faced human beings
how to be better undercover racists. I
am tired of the vilifying stares from
citizens, politicians, academics and
public intellectuals who have never
slept a night with Black and Brown
dreams!

FIRST LOVE

opened my eyes one afternoon
on the stoop like waking from a
dream, the weight of gravity in
the South Bronx bending me with
laughter, you circling toward the
steps with the wind, music playing
. from an open window of a second
story apartment and I could not explain
to myself what makes the sugarcane in
the bodega on the corner remarkably
sweet. how strange that I was lost for
words while thinking the stars are in
love with the evening sky, pigeons
on the fire escapes facing the avenue
with each other and the fairest image of
you sending flowers to my twelve year
old lips to kiss you. if you could be
with me on the stoop today I would
whisper many years of the sweetest
things in your girlish ears to confess
the time I loved you.

CÉSAR CHÁVEZ

standing in fields with farmers
hands, he did for many what

seemed impossible and taught
the world to say ¡Sí, Se Puede!

he resisted in peaceful ways the
owners of farms who put food

on tables harvested by the least
regarded human beings. you César

Chávez crossed the boundaries
of religion, gender, class and race

in the name of the right of the poor
to organize for fair wages, clean

water and safe places of work. you
believed DDT should never fall from

the sky on the heads of laborers who
are used until they are not needed

and then left to fall into graves. today,
we remember your tireless acts in a

troubled world for the cause of people
without rights, wretched farmers of

the earth and strikes that finally even
cost your life. we weep for you with

eyes gone dry and believe like you we
are on earth to build a life of justice in

which the poor who work the land
that feeds all of us can breathe peace.

SUNDAY

these are the voices heard for
certain once each week, trusted
to convey something of the truth
of heaven on earth, echoing in us
when we walk in the darkness, step
over cracks on the city sidewalk, sigh
at the sight of tenements vacant before
they fall and that never say quite enough
to save us. these are the manicured and
puzzling preachers, the chosen who talk
mostly about their spins, whose eyes
hurry over the Bible pages to the next
admired text and who pretend to see the
wretched poor that dress up each week
to attend church. these are the men and
women who have no idea sleep for us is
never about counting sheep but always
of crossing borders with big walls, evading
armed cops and white vigilantes God never
stops. these are the people that need to hear
us talk about being waist deep in the river,
life in the barrio, workplace, schoolyard,
courts, Lilly white worship houses and the
lynching fields.

POLITICIANS

they are in it for themselves
he would say after taking a
noisy sip of café, never for the
junkies sleeping in the park
or the poor looking between
jobs for signs of hope. I only
nodded thinking about those
living on the block compared
to the long tally of the departed
seen off at the Ortiz Funeral Home
on First Avenue. they have no real
interest in our loud screams, our fists
raised in the air, the color of our
skin, languages spoken in the barrio
or the flowers planted by Abuelas by
the river adorning the edges of this
neighborhood where we all find so
much comfort in the dark. I looked
up nodding with interest and could
see light pouring from his mouth and
closing in on the politicians making empty
promises. whatever else happened that
morning, I confess being overcome with
a need to pray though it would likely not
serve to change the life too precious
for us.

THE STROLL

I walked the four long blocks
to the East River waving que
pasa to the people living with
lost time in their shanty town
lot, catching the voices from a
chorus pouring onto the street
from the Pentecostal church in
the middle of the block on 4th
Street, carrying the beautiful dark
faces shaking me full of God's own
joy and amused by the crumbling
buildings that spell our names. I
strolled breathing in sofrito smells
calling me home, pausing for a few
minutes with the viejos proposing
toasts with beer in bags in front of
Joey's bodega, thankful for their old
world spiritual clarity that will never
be cheapened by academics coughing
up questions that cannot raise Brown
children from the dead. finally, I
reached the river, sat on a splintered
tree log to watch the current and sank
into stillness, while on a bench next
to me three men played congas.

GOOD NEWS

I walked down the avenue in
a trance imagining that the mural
on the wall was drawn by the hands
of grandmothers on the block under
the watchful eyes of children who
finally sat still. I listened to the old
women say they drew on the side of
the building to say heaven was never
finished and the candles lit in church
will keep us from becoming familiar
with the darker side of things. I am
surprised by nothing now and often
join widows to pray for good news to
come.

CHANGO

Friday is for the
Santeria meeting on
Intervale Avenue to
listen to an African
God speak to us in
Spanish. we will
see Chango moving
in the room with drums
stirring the white dressed
priestess representing the
God with a place on the
altar of mother's Catholic
Saints. perhaps, after tonight's
meeting in the storefront
that used to be a barbershop
run by old men life will change
for us. perhaps, we will
look up at the moon and drag
it over the dark streets until
there is only light for us. after
a couple of hours with our
Yoruba God we may slip
into clarity and find reason
to hope.

VIOLENCE

every day I wonder why
there is too little objection
to the cars plowing through
a human rights crowd and
the heads that turn away
from the children shot in
schools? the silence about
the standing rules of hate,
the tolerance for violence,
the tragedies of gunfire, the
damaged lives stacked with
grief and those unrighteous
politicians demanding a new
civil war which are things to
make God weep. nowadays,
we live encircled by callous
executioners who line their
pockets in a society that like
the earth is threatened with
extinction. I pray for more
days packed by kindness for
the darker children of the earth
and the presence of a God who
faced the perils of the Cross in
the name of everyone and thing
worth the high price of it.

SPANGLISH

this language that has been
given to us too many years
ago will never stop carrying us
each day, offering phrases not
to forget and rising as well some
day from the inner-city graves.
these Spanglish words that have
been good enough for prayer, the
sound of living and the whispers
of love will get us into heaven to
forget how we dragged ourselves
across the desert, urban streets, and
cheap work. these words that have
cleverly slipped through the grammar
cracks will be for us on earth and in
heaven.

DIFFERENT

you have not told me what
makes you different, is it

you have never worked in
fields harvesting strawberries

with planes spraying pesticide
above your head, perhaps your

nails perfectly cut and shined
are always free of dirt, maybe

you think your white hands are
the right color to keep you from

rassling for life. I learned from
American history that people like

you delighted by equality speeches
think Black is not beautiful and

corn-made foreign language and
Spanglish speakers are just way too

brown to have around. you have
not said anything about the ways

people like me built this nation, instead
you are silent about what people on

my side of the tracks endure in your
America. what makes you different

is not your fictive white superiority,
instead it is that culture of cruelty

you live each day to bring misery to
dark-skinned human beings.

BORICUA

I was told many years ago
by old women who dusted

Saints in church that God
loved me though knowing

deadly years on city streets
and village fields it occurred

to me that may have been true
in Eden. the mocking laughter of

America has been louder in my
Puerto Rican ears than summer

days with singing crickets and
longer than the lines we make

to beg the makers of indelicate
speeches in Congress to treat us

equally. I have seen lynching
rope etched with Spanish names

in our different kind of life, God
bitterly questioned, while nothing

on earth can keep us from resisting
every sword made in the USA that

deserve shattering into contemptible
pieces.

SCHOOL BOY

he was a public school boy
who rode the city bus with

a weekly pass. his skinny
body was the universe of

mystery into which were
poured lessons from the

world that argued with the
rejects full of love-stricken

barrio dreams. when in the
school auditorium each day

he pledged allegiance to the
flag as radiators hissed and

Spanish voices feel silent.
sometimes, waiting with the

moon light on tenement roof
tops, while recalling things,

he wondered why new days
never begin with the things

people are missing. I can still
see his block with the blinking

traffic light, the faces on it
in Black and Brown beauty,

the splendid gaze in the boy's
eyes and times on the stoop,

plainly.

THE PROMISE

no one has tried to tell
us what God felt looking

upon creation. no one argues
with the scribes taking note

of the brutal obscenities of
the country and the eyes so

tightly shut in the church. no
one objects to the bards who

write barrio love poems, keep
a candle burning when lights

are out and keep us in faith
when Spanglish lives hastily

perish. no one still believes
the prayers of priests have

privileges in heaven, speak
for people receiving crippled

wages and crying out to the
distant bastion of God in a

language English churches
do not understand. everyone

questions the idea that we are
the children of God, the heirs to

divine promises, the younger
siblings of a jobless crucified

middle-eastern savior, and a
people on earth made in the

image of the divine. perhaps,
the public on the other side

of the river full of sin needs
to hear that bullshit.

THE SURPRISE

on the River Walk in San Antonio
wrapped up in the sights and the
world that gives me life, watching
boats move along the water, I got
tickets for the family river boat ride
and was given one by a vendor marked
seniors. I must admit the seller's
assumption startled me leaving me
with the need to say no I was not
around when the light-bulb was
invented and a senior has not yet
exploded in my greying head. I had
run ten miles that morning realizing
the any new activity that emerged
for me was being called something
I never felt and it made me think about
how to get off the express train to catch
the local. the next day, I could almost hear
Auden whisper grace before eating and saw
within me the printed word in his poem
doggerel advising me to keep chaos at
arm's length. I will do my best until it is
time for a mind change into those blimey
golden years.

AWAKE

we have time to march into
the future with countless
stops.

the memories already fading
will last a few more years in
worked out dreams.

in the precious morning a new
day of hard work will sing us
from sleep.

a flaming sunrise will warm
today's sores to make sure we
reach other times.

THE BEGGARS

when the library is closed
you will find beggars in the
park drinking to forget the
world that has condemned
them to do time on the streets
until death parts them. they
comprehend the story of the
homeless punk kids squatting
in abandoned tenements on 3rd
Street, the old woman who stands
on the corner of Houston Street
with a paper cup selling the wrinkles
on her face a line at a time and even
the holiness of poverty. they greet
the neighborhood priest who leads
a pretty stained-glass window church
where the light of heaven rarely shines
and beggars are too smelly to occupy
a pew. these beggars lamenting the closed
library know exactly how to bless bread
and wine with dirty hands that hide God
in the flesh.

LOVE

love comes like an echo
pouring into me even in
darkest times. it comes to
me in dreams, leaping the
gates of heaven and with
cool chanting stories of
glossy truth. heart, I say
keep still for the moment
while the love that comes
takes my hand. love comes
to me outside the silent
church and says when I
discern divine words attend
to the world and pray mercy
for it.

WHITMAN

morning began offering the
same little life that dragged
us back to the public school
that did not speak Spanish
and that promised no future
for the kids sharing secrets
on the playground in their
foreign tongue. we attended
classes all day dying in them
a little more by the end of the
week and never offered flowers
by teachers with voices that were
seldom sweet. Whitman would
have answered our questions like
he did the child who asked what
is grass. in the classroom, the poet
would have paid attention to every
voice, tongues expressing Spanish
and kids shouting broken English
dreams. you know instead of grass,
we asked what is a Palm tree and can
they grow in the South Bronx?

OLD MAN

old man wearing the rosary
around your brown neck known
well by the children dashing the
streets, busily sorting the displaced
memories erupting to mind of time
beside the ocean, each year a little
more alone and missing the kindness
of aged departed friends, you told me
they never leave your presence. old
man, the world looks in on you, smiles
with you, rests in your creaky rooms,
plays with you like you were a young
schoolboy and even breathes heavy with
you after slow walks. old man, we could
hear the roaring rainy season wind calling
you, saw your face glow more radiantly
than the aging sun, listened to the living
words that fell from your lips and in this
place and time chuckled when they gently
delivered us to mysterious Eden. old man,
you are seldom full of sleep and daily you
roam deeper into a faith that carries you
up the mythological river bathing Central
American lands.

THE CONFIRMATION

I was looking at the fruit
dangling in the color green
from a mango tree and saw
parakeets nesting on their
secret spot waiting perhaps
for a sky full of stars. we
spent the afternoon with all
the ghosts who shouted on
the streets and went to war
to protest suffering, the elders
who had seen too much, the
peasants with permanently
blistered hands, the widows
and children standing tall in
divine light. we gathered at
the edges of the city to wait
for the patient stories from
the familiar margins, curse
evil at its core wherever it
takes possession of human
bodies and to revel beside the
mango tree with witnesses
who rehearsed with accurate
memories the messages that
give us life, even while tears
try their best to hold up the
messy world.

SORROW

I was born on this land
without a drop of hate,
learned to smile at its
many colored faces till
with my darker brothers
and sisters white faced
citizens maimed, raped
and killed us and shouted
you are not American. the
point-blank shooters who
desecrate the ballot box of
democracy deny that Black
lives matter and Brown people
have always been around. at
night, when the devil appears
in sleep, we see the evil being
clapping for all the repugnant
white nationalists and legislators
who throw hate at churches, schools,
playgrounds and private homes to
try to keep justice from coming for
them.

KINDNESS

when I think of the most
important noun one can
find in any Holy book it
occurs to me that word is
kindness. this enchanted
term will never leave you
vulnerable, always takes you
to understanding and away from
the violence in the world that
makes a waste of mysterious
and precious life. in the very
places any one of us lives, it is
clear that kindness saves us from
savage days and nourishes more
than money, fear and hate. the
word leads me to think of holding
the hand of the sick, the battered,
the lonely, the dying and the earthly
witnesses to the justice that comes
with promises of peace. the last
time I sat in San Oscar Romero's
church, I recalled that kindness was
for him the essence of the gospel
and the surest way to live out the
meaning of woke.

ODDS

I have played the odds long
before horses were gambled
at off track betting in Manhattan.
I have played the odds standing
on the corner when cops from the
41st Precinct came by to knock me
to the ground for being a spic or
in the time of mixing sorrow with
the days spent in school learning
things that put knots in my Puerto
Rican stomach. I played the odds
in the church that forgot my name
after baptism and on streets with
violence that splits skin open. I have
played the odds holding the hands
of dying friends, weeping for a dead
brother and listening to life stories told
by people with crushed dreams. I have
played the odds praying for injustice to
end and God to come down to the barrio
to shout our Spanish names.

TONIGHT

there are no strangers
on the streets tonight,
no documents to show
on the sidewalks, not a
sign of lost love in the
shadows, just warm wind
blowing from the north
shouting Jesus and truth
made flesh way down in
forgotten places. tonight,
pain is sweet so you best
start singing the everlasting
songs written by the wretched
of the earth that America still
wants enslaved.

THE DIVORCE

once collected you
think of that home
with dingy windows,
kids' beds and a big
wood table. the voices
of parents have faded
into a room of childhood
memory, easy whispers
of remarkable days and
then the unexpected coldness
of divorce we know left you
changed. but you young
woman, wait for light to
fill you and perhaps even
look to heaven for change.
in the hours you should
know this is no less a time
of love and even the shadows
care for you more on sad days
than any God could ever in
life imagine.

TOSSING LINES

we sit in the park like flags
blown by the wind waiting
for a little mana to fall from
the sky, today. we look for
signs in the clouds that will
announce the exact time the
Savior comes to abolish death
and the habits misinterpreting
regular life. the daylight has
gone out of its way to wake
us from gracious sleep and
we smile at the group of old
Spanish speaking women walking
in front of the stoop announcing
with each step and their watchful
eyes that they prefer light. our long
Spanglish sentences again cannot
understand the country that offers
us less than half a life and we settle
the confusion by telling jokes that
unburden us and helps us wait for
heaven to clear.

THE HOSPITAL

Lincoln hospital was called the butcher
shop by the Puerto Rican kids brought
into the world in its operating rooms.
the place was founded in the 1830 by
the Society for the Relief of Worthy
Aged Indigent Colored Persons. the
hospital later called The Colored Home
and Hospital officially became known
by its presidential name in 1902, located
in the South Bronx and by the 1970s it was
taken over by the Young Lords for failing
to serve the health needs of the Black and
Brown poor. I was born in Lincoln Hospital,
the place student doctors with white faces
fresh from the suburbs were never quite sure
of clinical facts and nearly always misunderstood
their broken english and dark-skinned patients
who had a new universe of needs. as a young
boy taken to the emergency room, I recall a
room full of faces saturated by sadness and
those were the people not ill. the white coats
dashing around the halls and into rooms seemed
to me rather near-sighted to the bruises on the
Puerto Rican knees from kneeling on them day
and night, while the landlords, factory owners,
and white politicians with their world of secrets

took high tea! the image of single mothers with
infants and elderly women fumbling the beads
on their Rosaries followed me for years on the city's
sonorous sidewalks, crowded subways and across
many worlds where I improvised life. perhaps,
I should be thankful for coming into the world in
a butcher shop where my Puerto Rican mother could
not tell heaven from earth.

THE BEACH

the ocean has been coming ashore
ever since the first carried memory
waded on the sandbar and hosted like
today playful children. on these Orchard
Beach days some wondered what Noah
thought about a world covered with water,
others that the darkness could not prevent
the light from sticking to them, kids about
combing the beach for discarded bottles
to turn in for deposits and abuelas with wet
ankles of the many faces of God. on weekends,
the neighborhood made its way to the waters of
the Long Island Sound where sofrito people
peered out to sea and swam in each other for
hours. no one ever complained of losing the
day in Salsa songs, Brown bathers shouting
Spanish from the receding surf or children in
their circus games chattering in any tongue
they wished. on Orchard Beach days no one
could be reached by the evening news and
you could hear people whispering into the
wind, perfect!

SALVATION

I wanted to be startled
by governors weeping
for children murdered
in schools, to believe a
nation in prayer would
split shooters' darkness
with light and find those
on the mourner's bench
joined by others against
evil. I weep for the spilled
blood of children, grieve
for the teachers who tried
to protect them, and plead
for the welcome voice of
God not heard by those too
much in love with guns.

WHEN I THINK OF THEM

they heard the frightened voices
of children on 911 calls, like the
kids some of them would go home
to hug and they let the minutes tick
away with their special smell of the
burning of hell. they waited longer
than all the shots fired, dressed in
fresh uniforms with shiny badges
ready to punish devasted parents
in the name of a police code too
dark for the innocent inside of the
school building to survive. we are
left thinking about all the loss, the
classrooms where blood was spilled
with bodies beyond recognition that
will remain ripe with decay longer
than life itself. we have counted the
tiny broken bodies, the spots of God
left in an elementary school prayer
cannot make whole. we rage at the
end of life for those with too little
experience to measure and the coffins
receiving them. at each graveside, we
stare at the sheltering earth that weeps
about the gun violence moving across
her sacred body.

LISTEN

you who are called the
latest martyrs of the old
church heard the report
of gun shots that echoed
in an elementary school
building like the bell that
clanged with bullets at the
Cathedral. you who hear
the faces split with tears,
the wicked shooters words,
his mother's prayers to God
in heaven and the last words
of teachers who sheltered kids
too young to think about their
lives in their arms before they
perished. you who watched
from heaven the bullets that
changed the tiny bodies, the
gun that did not care to learn
Spanish names, the wrong
time and place that will be
with us for life, know the hell
we live each day on earth. you
who hear us ask where is God
in the madness, in creation with
so many turns of violence and

when the door in heaven stays
closed. listen, heal the despairing
and lead us to salvation on this
earth!

THE LOVERS

they stand on the subway platform
holding hands, passing with kisses
lipstick between their lips, looking
up at each new rider joining them at
the 59th Street station, speaking softly
in each other's ear, while their lover's
eyes prance around the station. they
have promised each other more days
full of dreamy hope, startling moments
of delicious mystery and the bright days
only love can fully explain. they share
the platform with the sound of Andean
music they spy on the downtown side of
the tracks, a homeless man doing push ups
where the waiting sidewalk ends with a
backpack full of worldly things neatly
placed against the wall and beneath the
mosaic that reads Columbus Circle, which
will delight no doubt future archeologists
hundreds of years from now. the couple
no longer whispers but looks at the light
cutting the tunnel dark, feeling the wind
made by the first rushing car and allowing
their beautiful dark faces to drift now into
the deepest spaces of the ancient songs that
awaken their souls.

NEVER

everyone leaves home they
told me on the windy walk to
New York from the tiny village
where grandmothers blessed us
by gently touching our heads,
right before their hands turned
into birds to lead the long way
north. I will never leave home,
the days of screaming laughter,
the moral lessons tested by too
much darkness and the times when
the hate that came knocking from
the country of blood-stained money
was finely rejected. I will never
leave home where we turned books
wrong side out to learn the truth the
white kidnappers of history refused
to write and when pushing against the
terror of America's blindness.

THE STORY TELLER

the world was too much with
us in the late winter of the South

Bronx, cold and wet. in a room
too small for three kids we

heard stories that migrated to New
York from Guatemala that were not

like Charlotte's Web. one truly dark
night on a walk that required crossing

a long bridge a veiled woman who came
out of a thicket of corn walked toward

my father whose feelings were by then
choking his throat. she asked for directions

to the village, then the old man described
a brutal silence, the veil coming off and

the woman rolling across the bridge in a
ball of fire before shooting up the side of

a tree and blowing up louder than a first
burst of thunder, la Llorona! we stayed

up late listening in the old tenement to
pop telling us stories and through the thin

walls we heard more of people who came
from years of cutting sugar cane, picking

coffee, harvesting lettuce and recalling
how they were once children who swarmed

in schoolyards, soccer fields, at Sunday
mass and places where they talked story

after story about going north to get a very
different taste of hope. eventually, story

time ended though we would turn over to
sleep inflated with suspicion about father's

world of mysteries!

.

LOVE

if I had a lantern I would
rub it on this entrancing night
to wish only to sit across from
you somewhere we had never
been and imagine together God's
love touching ground from far away
heaven offering blessings lost on
every Sunday that would only remind
us of the noisy days torn by years of
civil war. if the lantern gave me three
wishes I would use the last two first
to ask to keep this moment without end
and then finally to stretch desire across
the Mesoamerican earth in the name of
the first day we met.

MESSIAH

God became time in undocumented
flesh to carry our names, stories,
villages, joys, scars, native tongue
and Spanglish words. every day God
evicted from church is more illegal,
wrinkled by the prayers of a migrant
earth, weeping for the houses ripped
to pieces by calling upon heaven to
help them become better at surviving.
God is dark bodies wrapped in graves,
the movement between two worlds, waking
up in the languages of the street, loved
ones begging for bread, an undivided
house and a lynched human being.

SUNDAY

a thick flock of pigeons is
casually gathered in the
park some on grass with
dew that glistens in the
rising sun. the quiet Sunday
with a perfect sky devising
mystical moments is how God
might be imagined, simple and
without words. the pure breeze
blowing across these old benches
may allow us to question conceited
piety in church and preachers who
are expensively dressed and think
God has squandered grace on people
in need.

MYSELF

I live in a country that freed
itself from the tyranny of an
English king but cannot find
a more perfect union nor state
of liberty. I spend my days
with people who have walked
more than once to Jerusalem
and back, have settled in strange
cities, take long walks in parks
filled with the sound of multiple
languages and are lined by trees
aged in perfect green. the poets
I read have been with me longer
than time known with my childhood
family. whenever I roam the New
York sidewalks or pause to watch
the pigeons pacing on the fire escapes
I find myself trying to understand
the sweet brevity of life and some
days even the imprecise truth in the
work of theologians. I cannot recall
the sound of my brother's voice who
I buried too young nor stop wondering
if our paths will cross in that place the
preachers call, heaven.

BIRTH

I was born crying in a
city hospital though no
one imagined it was not
from the shock of birth.
my eyes were found by
my mother's tears who
saw her suffering people
working hard and kids
from the block taking
their poor thin bodies to
school and at least twice
a year to church. the first
few days in the hospital
the sweet lady who gave
me life could not figure
out why a tiny pool of
tears were stuck in each
of my eyes but I did not
have the words to say you
put them there to prepare
me for a world that would
find thousands of ways to
curse me out. I confess to
being surprised sometimes
that there are tears left but
I suppose that too came from

my minimum wage mother
who said in perfect broken
English recuerda life is a
blessing!

ROADSIDE

we have not disputed that the
desert has stretched across the
State melting with its inferno
heat everything in its way. a
tractor trailer was abandoned
when the sun came out to make
us tremble and fifty-three souls
perished in it leaving the world
penetrated by horror. the silence
left now to us threatens the spaces
visited in the name of God while
demanding that justice for human
beings who searched for a better
way of life be pressed from the
face of involved nations. sadly, it
will happen again dissolving the idea
that a Christian country offers all
a haven or maybe it will shatter
the thought these deaths and human
trafficking have nothing to do with
us. sadly, these undocumented dead
will unlikely make the country say to
others come live with us.

WISE

I have greyed with forgotten
children, the Spanglish kids

seen with suspicion, treated
like gangsters, thrown in jails

for crimes not committed and
failed by schools. some of us

have written with ink on naked
skin sweetly improvised dreams,

the identity of shredded lovers
and names of fallen kin. we have

greyed waiting for the savior to
hold us with healing hands, raise

the dead and make the cruel see
but our Black and Brown faces

with a few more wrinkles still
walk in a world that scarcely

loves us. on the crippled block
we remember to gather despite

it all cause happiness shouts around
us without a lick of English, just

like church bells ringing on Sunday
and in the space's supremacists think

they are too good to visit. we laugh
about the plague sent to get us that

cannot finally kill us!!

THE CATHEDRAL

bad weather shut the roads
in the park much like those
in the woods Kipling wept
though carefully observing
he noticed hints of paths. it is
easy to make your way into
the park by going over the.
barriers and walking along
the wet paths that lead you
to dearest solitude that many
have never known. this is not
the place of a lost road nor of
diverging paths in a yellow
wood, in Spanish Harlem we
call it the place found that no
matter where you walk gives
some sort of beautiful for you
to notice. when you sit alone
you can hear the wind carrying
the gentle whistle of the urban
afternoon, the sounds of distant
sirens, the laughter of children
on the West Side playgrounds
and sometimes you can even
imagine howling wolves. you
will be lifted into a new world

of thoughts in that little section
of the park, taken away from the
mighty days of political division,
and placed on the route you now
wonder why you were afraid to
walk. did I ever tell you the
park has been my Guadalupian
Cathedral since I first slept it
on a bench by the Bethesda
Fountain?

GUN SHOTS

we have waited for years
for the reckoning, a time

of coming revelation, a
simple word that makes

darkness flee and pitiless
violence end. generations

have questioned the slow
legs of justice, centuries

of denial and the divine
retreat from a world that

begs for a second coming.
we now measure grief by

the minute, dress with the
contemporary style of the

Cross, see the wounds on
each other's hands and

cry for the balm that will
restore smiles to terrified

faces. how long will life
be like a broken glass that

cannot collect tears? when
will the saccharine prayers

for the innocent who died
stop their chattering in the

air? how many burials
will it take? will memories

of the dead that float forever
in us ever lead to a glimpse

of heaven?

LANGUAGE

words make different sounds
on human lips that come from
every corner of the big world
soaked with magnificent kinds
of accumulated knowledge and
experience. you may disagree but
language you see is the original
caravan that carried people to stole
indigenous land, it is the migrant
gossiper practiced in the fabled
noises of European tongues, the
ocean crossing speech of nations
that traversed borders and settled
on a novel piece of earth brushed by
the wind that for thousands of years
never blew across valleys, woods,
rivers or mountains a Spanish or
English word. in these Americas
European words for more than 500
years have enslaved, battered, raped,
killed and occupied the land and all
people on it.

THE SINGER

the velvet, smooth, liquid
voice of Nat King Cole is
singing with impeccable pitch
in the café hurrying listeners
in the room on this hot day to
their own stardust lyrics. no
one has vacant eyes catching
the sounds made by the baritone
with a gift never intended for
small rooms. stars climbing
high up into the sky begin to
inspire people to tell stories
about you know yesterdays
loves. for the price of a few
more conversations, I will try
not to let the reverie of these
enchanting men and women
slip away into a lonely night
of fairytales that never dream
a flowered paradise reaches
us just like Cole sings and always
in our hearts that are ready for
love's dearest refrain. perhaps, by
the end of the song no one will
ache quite the same tonight and
a kiss will be no less a mythic
inspiration.

BELIEVE

we have waited
      several lifetimes
for
      the fragmented
world
to
  change
    to enter
a
  world
    where
justice
    is
      wide awake.
we
never
    think defeat
but wonder
how
      long will it take
for uplifting
         light
to make its
way
    down here?

THE RIGHTIST

the media clings to its
sensational reporting
of hypocrisy coming
from the rickety lips
of rightist politicians
who love to say lots of
prayers after shootings
to a god who finds time
to condescend to the
poor, the vulnerable
and deported. in the
halls of Congress, they
amuse themselves by
repeating homilies with
hateful words they toss
over the wall from their
heaven. the news media
reports they also find ways
to applaud the white rage
putting signs on Black and
Brown bodies saying, "shoot
me!" the rest of us wake up
tired and fed up with a country
that pushes its weight to make
us fugitives and fatalities of
their racist empire.

EYES OPEN

one day we will find written
in heavenly script words that
lead to a deep pounding in the
chest and away from blindness
to the weeping for the endless
requirements of love. soon, if
there is a Crucified God that
listens, we will tell stories to
the Saints about the inventory
of earth-covered death spread
by empires that are oblivious
to a God who leans down with
dreams that are placed on the
mountains that no one any longer
expect to move. one day, we will
emerge from the murky shallows
into the grandeur of a simple day
leaping with the unimaginable
sight, smell and touch of the
first and absolute reality that
is clearly God sighing one last
time in Golgotha!

THE BIBLE

before reading your
reverse standard Bible
that tells you another
story of a God who puts
out the lights, I want to
remind you the dead
like feathers are carried
to the places your faith
ignores. you dear servants
who read false words and
plead ignorance of the cries
on this noisy earth should
know the God you never
find in the book you prize
remembers every name
you despise. in the beautiful
world sustained by approving
love and unsteady worldly
kindness God dropped in to
give us the light you never
held, fool! remember this
when you have your next
confused Bible reading hour
to make foul interpretations
that never disclose the guiding
star of Bethlehem.

SAVED

the day light stretches
into night outside of
the shop selling Saints,
portions and carvings
of African gods. the
fatherless boys play
tag on the street like
nothing else matters and
Hank exits an abandoned
building where he shot dope
talking to himself. the local
priest carrying a dry cleaned
robe walks quickly toward
his church where his life work
is saved without blessing from
the block. Nena who is sitting
on the stoop watches the nothing
to do with me priest hurry passed
her thinking God should read a
few pages of the unabridged Bible
used on the block to understand
why so many people complain
in this corner of the world that
truth in the good book sets no one
free.

DEMOCRACY

democracy is quite ill
with the South raising
more followers of the
lost cause and the North
saying too little about
lynching trees. streets
mature daily around the
country with screams
from dark bodies beaten
and killed to make the
nation whiter than
yesterday. what color
is democracy created by
trickery and idol worship
fools? what color is the
endless flow of division
that mocks God's work
while elected criminals
figure out how to issue
identity cards to people
who stand on lines and
never hear their names
called. what is the meaning
of white for a democracy
driven to its knees and
bleeding like a tenement
dripping faucet?

MEDITATION

alone in the garden on a
hot summer morning I
count birds timing how
often they visit while the
dog sleeps. I give each
of them a Spanish name
and listen to their warm
freedom songs. I sit silent
trying to decipher the chants
of these feathered creatures
and feel they mischievously
smile.

WAITING

on the long road back to
the edge of the world where
everyone lives in Spanish
and store front churches
spend hours calling on God
with invented tradition, I
confess never speaking in
tongues and questioning in
this time of endless night
the second coming.
Tito invited me tonight
to wait with him for the
disclosing moment when
the preacher on Avenue
D will exit Mass like Lela
slipped out of the party in
Apartment 5C and life will
not assault us. we looked
down the street at the stray
dog we called lucky that
ran into an alley laughing
while time ran its course
and our mute God broke
promises in the world that
makes us mourn.

THE RIVER BANK

these women have cried to us
on the river bank they reached
after circling graves in villages
left. they have come carrying
crosses around their necks and
armed with the expectation that
decency would treat them well
across the border. they sit beside
the flowing water filling it with
tears that will keep dripping from
their eyes until the English clocks
stop ticking in the world that never
sees them. perfectly voiceless these
women have something to say about
writing history, who inherits the earth,
and being nonwhite females until death
parts them. I have been in crowded rooms
with them silently listening to how they
fill each other up and say the Angels
will met them to crumble the barriers
keeping their messages out of range,
joining them to set fire to histories of
hate and marching calmly with them
to places where men do pay for their
sins.

REMEMBERED

I don't have to tell you
dear brother in heaven
about junkies hanging
on the stoop nodding
into dreams, talking of
the old days when they
played round up tag on
the block before being
thrown away kids. the
day the apartment door
closed behind us home
you know became the
abandoned building on
the street with twisting
shadows mother never
walked. I bet you would
say we howled the lonely
nights, cursed the kick to
the streets and I must tell
you in prayers I do hope
reach you that I still grieve
that you died on Walton
Avenue, alone. you know,
I only have one picture of
you and the sound of your
voice dear brother is too

distant to make out though
that singular picture of you
when a child I cherish. I
journey at least once each
day into the darkness to
find you leaving a trail of
tears behind me to find my
way back out. I know you
remember what we have
seen together and I promise
to open my eyes a little wider
to clearly see the signs you
may be sending me about
how to remake paradise.

THE LOVERS

I walked the Mexican beach
today pausing to take in the
flight of pelicans next to the
lovers with the finest smiles
on the shoreline with silence
on their lips telling the story
of how they give themselves
to each other for eternity and
a week. I cannot walk into
the night without carrying
their inexhaustible image with
me and thanking each star for
their endless witness to what
dazzles life.

THE ANNOUNCEMENT

one evening when cold
winds could not overcome
the distance between the
citizens, walls appeared
to crumble, and the years
of alphabetized disasters
were nearly forgotten the
delusional politician that
the prayers of many have
not made change once again
stepped forward to assault a
weakened nation that cannot
hold on to the future with his
orange laughter. in these very
treacherous times the Bibles in
all the homes are upside down
and democracy certainly again
grotesquely marches toward its
own rope swing end. on this
Autumn night, we think about
protected white privilege hiding
in every word uttered by modern
America's two-faced trust fund
son who is blessed with the most
alarming blindness that lawmakers
appear to adore. who will save us

from this traitor's scheming when
prosecutors themselves go belly
up to not counter truth?

THE CRYING

the politics on these shores is
not without evil, the cooperation
of violence, the regular deliverance
of distorting lines and contempt for
the weary who wait for sweet chariots
to swing low. the cruelty that comes like
blowing wind in this place called home
piles up to make neat walls that hide the
faces of those who live with unendurable
suffering in all the places politics spreads
a white sheet of silence. the politics in my
beloved country hardly ever talks about all
it has abandoned, the criminals we share in
office and the hoarse voices speaking against
the loud silence. in these darkest times, the
offenders run for public office, prosecutors
action on the law vacillates to not change a
thing for the privileged and unlawful rich
and we are called upon to tame the hideous
monsters by adapting to them. with Dubois
we ask Christ to pity the toiling land and
I you must understand too often agree with
him that politics in America is two parties
at the service of the same evil.

CLUB Q

beloved afraid of living on these
shores for unapologetically loving
those who place a kiss on your cheek
despised by bigots who know nothing
of the embracing heart of God, you are
the rushing waters of the river that takes
us to peek into another land that rejects
the self-righteous, errant theologians and
hateful killers who loathe the beauty in you
divinity made. tomorrow those who live in
places that wait for sudden and unexpected
messages from a heaven that balances all
kinds of love will sit with you at the same
banquet table finding in the lush talk around
it every rainbow dream that from the beginning
offered this divided world the most marvelous
things. let us chase the monsters who point the
barrels of their guns into hell and declare that
love is what saves this world and all of us now
in this time of grieving.